Don't Touch That Toad
& Other Strange Things Adults Tell You

WRITTEN BY
Catherine Rondina

ILLUSTRATED BY
Kevin Sylvester

KIDS CAN PRESS

With thanks to my editors, Sheila Barry and Lisa Tedesco. And a special thank you to my family, especially my "in-house" editor, my daughter Nella, who diligently read the manuscript over and over. — C.R.

First paperback edition 2014

Kids Can Press acknowledges the financial support of the Government of Ontario, through the Ontario Media Development Corporation's Ontario Book Initiative; the Ontario Arts Council; the Canada Council for the Arts; and the Government of Canada, through the CBF, for our publishing activity.

Published in Canada by
Kids Can Press Ltd.
25 Dockside Drive
Toronto, ON M5A 0B5

Published in the U.S. by
Kids Can Press Ltd.
2250 Military Road
Tonawanda, NY 14150

www.kidscanpress.com

The artwork in this book was rendered in ink
The text is set in Goudy and Whimsy.

Edited by Sheila Barry and Lisa Tedesco
Designed by Julia Naimska

The hardcover edition of this book is smyth sewn casebound.
The paperback edition of this book is limp sewn with a drawn-on cover.

Manufactured in Buji, Shenzhen, China, in 3/2014 by WKT Company

CM 10 0 9 8 7 6 5 4 3
CM PA 14 0 9 8 7 6 5 4 3 2 1

Library and Archives Canada Cataloguing in Publication

Rondina, Catherine
    Don't touch that toad & other strange things adults tell you / written by Catherine Rondina ; illustrated by Kevin Sylvester.

ISBN 978-1-55453-454-8 (bound)
ISBN 978-1-55453-455-5 (pbk.)

1. Superstition — Miscellanea — Juvenile literature. 2. Superstition — Miscellanea — Juvenile humor. 3. Folklore — Miscellanea — Juvenile literature. 4. Folklore — Miscellanea — Juvenile humor. I. Sylvester, Kevin II. Title.

GR81.R65 2010 j398'.41 C2009-906784-6

Kids Can Press is a **COrus**™ Entertainment company

Contents

Introduction

I'm sure you've heard a lot of
weird things over time from your parents,
your grandparents or even your teachers.
You'll probably find some of those sayings
here within these pages. Some of the
expressions will thrill you, some will make
you think, others will just gross you out,
but what you'll find really interesting is
where and how these crazy expressions got
started as well as how they've been passed
along from generation to generation.
What were those adults thinking?

Healthy Habits

Warning — this may be bad for you! Adults probably give more advice about your health than anything else. "Do this." "Don't do that." "Never try this." It's enough to make you sick just hearing all the parental dos and don'ts. Maybe the best health advice is "Don't listen to adults."

Cracking your knuckles can cause arthritis.

Are you the knuckle cracker making that disturbing noise? You probably think it sounds cool and even makes you look tough, but what are you doing to your hands? According to many adults, you could be setting yourself up for a serious case of arthritis. It's an illness that can cause pain and swelling in your joints, the places where your bones meet. And believe me, even your funny bone won't find it very amusing if you get arthritis.

FALSE

While it's been proven that cracking your knuckles won't give you arthritis, it's still not a handy exercise for your fingers. A study compared 74 people over the age of 45 who'd been knuckle crackers for decades with 226 people over the age of 45 who'd never cracked a single knuckle in their lives. The researchers found no differences between the hands that did and the hands that didn't. But the same study did reveal that knuckle cracking can cause a decrease in your ability to grip things. When you crack your knuckles, you're pushing the joints of your fingers in and out of their normal position and squishing the thick, clear liquid that helps keep the joints between your fingers lubricated. This pressure causes the knuckle bones to pull apart, which reduces the fluid in your joints and causes bubbles to form, expand and burst. Over time, all this bone popping and liquid loss can lead to a weaker grip. So try to think of something else to do with your fingers, such as picking your nose. Or just keep your hands to yourself and stop them from cracking each other!

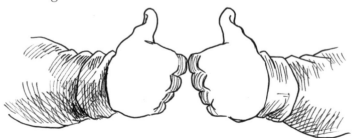

An apple a day keeps the doctor away.

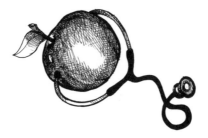

A is for apple,
B is for banana,
C is for … come on, give me a break.

Can a simple piece of fruit really keep you healthy?
Sure, apples have vitamin C, which is important for
keeping body tissues such as muscles and gums in
good shape. But do they have some secret ingredient
that turns regular human beings into super-healthy
droids? If there is any truth to this saying, maybe
you've underestimated the power of a slice of Mom's
apple pie.

FALSE

While apples are truly a fabulous fruit, loaded with all sorts of good things, they can't keep you from getting sick. But don't let this bruise your image of the crispy, yummy snack. It turns out eating apples has many other healthy benefits. Apples are a good source of fiber, contain vitamin C and are rich in flavonoids, which are natural chemicals that give plants their color and are also very good for your entire body. All these nutrients can help reduce the risk of certain types of cancer and heart disease. And there's also great news for those of you who like apples in liquid form. Researchers at the University of California have discovered that the juices found in apples can kill up to 80 percent of bacteria in your mouth, which is what causes tooth decay. So maybe the saying should be changed to "An apple a day keeps the dentist away."

If you play your music too loud, you'll go deaf!

You've probably heard your mom or dad telling you to "turn down your music or you'll go deaf!" But are your parents right? Can pumpin' up the volume on your favorite tunes really damage your ears?

TRUE

Yes, music lovers, you heard it right — now turn it down! Hearing loss can happen after you've been exposed to any loud noise over a long period of time. How loud is too loud? Well, sounds are measured in dB, which is a quieter way of saying decibels. Just kidding. Leaves rustling in the breeze are about 10 dB, a busy city street is around 90 dB. A car horn is about 110 dB, while a rock concert or a jet's engine can average between 110 and 130 dB! Most hearing loss due to loud noise is temporary, but anything above 85 dB can damage your ears permanently, especially if you're exposed to loud noise over a long period of time. Music fans who turn up the tunes might be hurting themselves without even realizing it. So the next time your parents yell at you to turn down the music, do as they say. Oh, and don't forget to remind them not to shout — it could damage your ears.

Don't eat raw cookie dough, or you'll get worms.

Your mom has just finished mixing a big batch of your favorite chocolate chip cookie dough. You're about to dip your finger into the delicious batter when she screams, "Stop! Don't eat that, or you'll get worms." Confused and a little angry, you move away from the mixing bowl, sulking. But could your mom be right? Could eating raw cookie dough really make you sick? Or is she only trying to scare you so she can have the batter all to herself?

Mom's right. It's best to wait and eat your cookies after they've been baked. If you eat the scrumptious raw cookie dough, you could get worms. Actually, these types of "worms" are really germs called salmonella, bacteria found naturally in the intestines of animals. If humans eat foods such as meat, chicken or eggs that contain salmonella, they can become very sick. Most people call it food poisoning, and it's not pretty. Symptoms can include stomach cramps, nausea, vomiting, diarrhea and fever. But not to worry, there's good news, too. By cooking these foods thoroughly, you can kill off the salmonella germs. The Canadian Food Inspection Agency recommends cooking eggs to at least 74°C (165°F). The other good news is that most premixed cookie dough is made safely with pasteurized eggs, which are cooked before they are put into the mix. So it's probably okay to scoop out a spoonful or two of that packaged cookie dough, as long as you read the label first.

If you go outside with wet hair, you'll catch a cold.

I know; it happens to the best of us. You're shampooing your locks when your dad screams, "Hurry, you've got five minutes until the bus comes!" But just as you're about to leave the house, you hear your mom yell, "Don't go outside with wet hair; you'll catch a cold." You can't really catch a cold by going outside with wet hair, can you?

FALSE

Don't be a drip, Mom — it's not true. When it comes to avoiding a cold, it's more important to wash your hands than it is to dry your wet hair. A cold is actually a virus, and viruses don't care if your hair is wet or dry, or if it's hot or cold outside. You can catch a cold only from direct contact with someone who already has one. Doctors believe that colds are more common in the winter not because of the temperature, but because we tend to stay inside for longer periods of time, where germs breed all around us. Still, you might want to dry your hair before you go outside on a cold or chilly day. Even though you won't catch anything, the moisture in your hair can freeze and make you feel cold and uncomfortable, like Frosty the Snowman having a bad hair day.

If an earwig crawls in your ear, it will eat your brain!

If you're like most people, the thought of an earwig crawling anywhere near you probably sends a shiver up your spine. Perhaps it's the pincerlike prongs at the tail end of their bodies or the fact that they love to hide in humid places such as your shoes, your bathroom or your towel on a warm summer day. Or is it all the stories you've heard about earwigs crawling into people's ears and nesting in their brains?

You can take the cotton out of your ears. Earwigs won't be looking for new real estate inside your head anytime soon. And for that matter, they won't lay their eggs in there, and they definitely won't eat your brain. In fact, even if an earwig thought your ear had a welcome mat, it wouldn't get very far. While it's true that your ear might provide an ideal location for earwigs because they like to hide in warm, humid crevices, you have membranes and bones in your ear that would block them from burrowing into your head. So you don't have to wig out about earwigs anymore, since they're pretty harmless to human beings. But I'll bet you still don't want to find one lying next to your head on your beach towel. Ewwwww!

Don't swallow bubble gum because it takes your body seven years to digest.

Uh-oh, did you just swallow that wad of gum you were chewing? According to many bubble gum experts, namely your parents, this evil substance can stay in your stomach undigested for seven years or more. You've probably heard rumors of kids who had to have emergency surgery to remove the masses of undigested wads of gum from their bellies. But could it be true? Can bubble gum really stay in your stomach for seven years?

FALSE

Almost everyone has swallowed a piece of gum at sometime in his or her life, and practically no one has had to see a doctor because of it. While it's true that your stomach can't break down a piece of gum the same way it digests other foods, your digestive system can get it moving along in the right direction — south! Gum is made up of natural and synthetic ingredients, such as gum resin, preservatives, flavorings and sweeteners. Your body can absorb most of these ingredients, except for the gum resin. But your digestive tract will keep pushing it through your gut until it ends up coming out in a bowel movement. Now, don't get too excited. Even though it won't get stuck in your stomach for years to come, chewing gum can cause problems to your teeth. So try to chew only sugarless gum, and don't have more than one or two pieces a day. Oh, and when you're done — spit it out into the garbage!

Don't sit too close to the TV, or you'll ruin your eyes.

You're lying on your living room floor enjoying your favorite TV show. As you inch closer to the screen, anticipating the next action-packed scene, your dad yells, "Don't sit so close to the TV, or you'll ruin your eyes!" Never mind damaging your eyes, dear old Dad almost gave you a heart attack! So why would parents say such a horrible thing about an electronic box that gives kids so much joy?

FALSE

"It's hogwash," says Dr. Lee Duffner, a spokesperson for the American Academy of Ophthalmology. In his professional opinion, you can't cause any physical damage to your eyes by sitting too close to the TV screen. Your eyes have a special muscle called the ciliary (sil-ee-air-ee), which does an incredible job of changing the shape of the eyes' lenses. These lenses will change each time you focus on something. So if you're sitting too close to the TV, the muscles controlling the lenses will automatically change their shape to help your eyes focus. In fact, kids can sit closer to a TV set than adults can because their eyes can focus better on objects that are up close. But before you set yourself up in front of the TV for a marathon of your favorite shows, keep in mind that

watching too much TV can turn you into a couch potato — and experts still aren't sure what prolonged TV exposure does to your brain.

Eating too much sugar will make you hyper!

"No way," you protest as you try to hide that pack of jawbreakers in your back pocket. How could your favorite ingredient in everything from ice cream to cotton candy really make you hyper? Don't believe it? Climb down from the ceiling, and we'll find out if it's true or not.

FALSE

Yes, you read it right, sticky fingers. Sugar won't make you hyper. Go tell Mom that according to the Journal of the American Medical Association, their studies show that sugar does not cause children to be hyperactive. JAMA and  other medical experts conducted numerous studies with kids in which some were given sugar and others were given a sugar substitute. But they didn't reveal to the parents which kids had the sugar and which ones didn't. Turns out the kids all acted the same way, whether they had sugar or not. Many experts believe that if kids come home from a birthday party all hyped up, it's because they've been with their friends having fun, not because of what they've been eating. But you still shouldn't gobble down tons of candy. There is plenty of evidence proving that too much sugar in your diet can lead to obesity, diabetes and tooth decay.

Weird Science

Strange — but possibly true? From dining on dirt, to holding your breath, to headless sprinting chickens, this list of oddities will leave you wondering if there really is life on Mars. Maybe that's where these advice-giving adults come from!

Stop yawning, it's contagious!

Maybe you yawned while reading this saying. If you did, then you're fairly normal. Everyone yawns, including babies, kids, teenagers and adults of all shapes and sizes. Most animals do it, too. It takes an average of only six seconds to yawn, and it's easy to do. Open your mouth, let your jaw drop, suck in some air and then release it. Pretty simple, eh? But contagious? Try yawning in a room full of people and see what happens.

According to researchers at the State University of New York, about 40 to 60 percent of the population are prone to contagious yawning. Scientists used to believe yawning signaled that someone was tired or bored. Now they think that the purpose of yawning is to cool the brain to help it work more effectively by increasing the blood flow. But what's even more interesting is the reason we copy each other when we yawn. Scientists think that contagious yawning dates back to early humans, when groups of us would send yawning signals to each other to keep our tribe alert. So yawning is like a learned memory passed along from our ancient ancestors; it's a clever way of communicating with those around us. If you yawn right now, chances are others will follow, and it may just be ancient behavior that has passed on through history.

Lightning never strikes the same place twice.

If lightning, along with its crashing sidekick, thunder, isn't terrifying enough, think about the idea of it coming back for more. That's right, you see it hit once and think it's over — but surprise! There it is again. Then think about the likelihood of this happening. Weather experts say that lightning hits Earth about a hundred times every second. So, what's the chance of the same place or thing being hit twice? If you're a math wiz, you may already be calculating an answer. But if you've ever thrown a dart, a baseball or a football, then you know it's pretty hard to hit the same target twice. Or is it?

FALSE

The idea that lightning cannot strike the same place twice is shockingly incorrect. Just ask the employees of some of lightning's favorite targets. The Empire State Building in New York City gets hit at least 25 times a year, and the CN Tower in Toronto, Canada, gets zapped between 40 and 50 times annually. The Eiffel Tower in France is struck on a regular basis, too. In 1902, a lightning bolt caused enough damage that builders had to reconstruct 90 meters (300 feet) of the upper section of the tower. So, why do these buildings get hit so often? It's because lightning usually takes the easiest route from the clouds to the ground by using the tallest building or tallest tree. But it's not just buildings that get hit time and time again. Roy C. Sullivan, a U.S. park ranger in Virginia, was struck by lightning seven times and survived each hit. He holds the record, but I wouldn't get close enough to shake his hand if I were you — you might get a shock.

Don't do that! You could scare someone to death.

Imagine sitting in a movie theater with all your buddies, munching away on popcorn. Suddenly, the lights dim and the creepy music begins, making the hair on the back of your neck stand up and your heart pound a bit faster. You can feel the tension building all around you. Then, out of nowhere, the bad guy breaks through the door and appears larger than life on the screen. Your popcorn flies everywhere, as you — along with just about everyone else in the theater — scream in fear. But can you really be scared to death?

When your body feels fear or senses danger, a chemical change happens. This is often called the "fight or flight" response. Your heart will speed up as it's flooded with chemicals such as adrenaline from your nervous system, your muscles will prepare for action, your pupils will dilate and your bladder may even let go. Not to worry, these are all good reactions to have if you're about to defend yourself. But can you ever be so frightened that you are scared to death? "Yes, it is possible," says neurologist Martin A. Samuels, who has spent his life exploring sudden death cases. Samuels believes there is proof that under very specific circumstances, someone can be scared to death. So the next time you think about jumping out and scaring your friends, you might want to reconsider. If they're scared enough, the jolt of chemicals from their brains could physically damage their hearts, and in extreme cases, even cause death!

Holding your breath for 30 seconds will cure the hiccups.

Did you know that some cases of the hiccups have lasted for days, weeks, months and even years! Take for instance poor Charles Osborne. He had the hiccups for 68 years, from 1922 to 1990! But could something as simple as holding his breath for 30 seconds really have cured him?

This cure for stopping the hiccups is just one of many. Here are a few other popular remedies: Ask someone to scare you. Put a spoonful of sugar on your tongue. Drink water from the wrong side of the glass. Although most of these cures can work, they baffle medical science because no one really knows how or why. So the next question to ask is this: Where exactly do hiccups come from? It seems your diaphragm is the problem spot. It's the dome-shaped muscle in your chest that helps push air in and out of your lungs. Hiccups happen when your diaphragm gets irritated and spasms. Lots of things can irritate the diaphragm, such as eating too quickly, laughing too hard or feeling nervous. When your diaphragm spasms, it sends an irregular breath up and across your voice box, which causes you to make a silly hiccup sound.

So getting rid of the hiccups is all about helping your diaphragm return to its normal rhythm. After all, it's a major muscle involved in keeping you breathing, so you don't want it freaking out on you all the time.

If you brush your hair a hundred times a day, it will grow stronger.

"… ninety-seven, ninety-eight, ninety-nine, one hundred." Whew, that's a lot of brushing. Now, for the other side. "One, two, three …" Hold it right there, Goldilocks. What in the name of Rapunzel do you think you're doing? Who's got time to sit around brushing their hair one hundred times a day? Your head has over one hundred thousand hairs on it. Are you really going to pamper each and every strand? And what good will it do you, anyway?

FALSE

This hair-raising lie is enough to make you want to pull your hair out! According to experts, you should brush your hair only to style it, and never when it's wet! It all has to do with the root of the problem — your hair roots that is. They're underneath your skin, made up of a group of cells called keratin that form the protein that makes hair. Each root is inside a tiny tube, in your skin, called a follicle. As your hair grows, it pushes out of the follicle through your scalp. But once it pops onto the surface of your skin, the hair cells aren't alive anymore. So if you brush your hair too hard or too long, you can pull it right out of its follicles. Just remember, it's not the number of times you brush your hair that keeps it strong and shiny looking, it's the quality of the brush you use. Make sure that the bristles have "ball tips," which help move the brush easily through your hair without pulling on it. And buy a new brush every year! And by the way, the best way to get strong, healthy-looking hair is to eat a healthy diet. A nutritious diet is good for your whole body, even the hair on your head.

Humans use only 10 percent of their brains.

Could this be true? Are you really using only a small portion of your brain cells? If so, just imagine what you'll be able to do once you start using all of them! According to some very smart people throughout history, such as William James, who started the first psychology laboratory in the United States in 1874, and another smarty-pants named Albert Einstein, one of the greatest scientists of all time, we use only a very small part of our mental powers. But should we take their word for it?

FALSE

"The 10 percent myth is so wrong, it's almost laughable," says neurologist Barry Gordon, who studies brain activity at the Johns Hopkins University School of Medicine in Baltimore, Maryland. According to Dr. Gordon, our brains are active almost all of the time and we use virtually every part. Just think about it. Your brain is an organ in your body, just like any other organ. How well do you think your body would work if you used only 10 percent of your heart? Not very well; in fact, you'd be dead. So it seems as though the statements made by James and Einstein were probably misunderstood at the time. What James actually said was that "We are making use of only a small part of our possible mental and physical resources." Somehow that got turned into a wacky expression about how we use only 10 percent of our brainpower. So much for the 10 percent theory. Turns out this one's a no-brainer — which really would be scientifically impossible!

Everyone eats a peck of dirt before dying.

If you were like most little kids, you probably made a few mud pies. But it's a little weird that anybody would actually eat a mud creation. Even if you did decide to try your muddy recipe, wouldn't one bite be enough for your taste buds to freak out? Besides, we're not talking a little dirt here. A peck of dirt is about 7.5 liters (2 gallons) of the grainy brown stuff, which adds up to about 18 cereal bowls full. Now that's a lot of mud pie eating, if you ask me.

TRUE

Almost everything we eat is grown in the dirt, so it only makes sense that we ingest some during our lives. But don't let the fact that you eat dirt make you gag. It turns out that eating a peck of dirt over your lifetime may help keep you healthier. Kids who have early contact with things often found living in dirt such as bacteria, viruses and parasites may receive a boost to their immune system that prepares it for various germ attacks in the future. Now this doesn't mean you should go out and grab a handful of earth from your garden every morning for breakfast, but if a grain or two sneaks into your food once in awhile, there's no need to worry.

Chicken soup can cure the common cold.

Achoo! Gesundheit!

Uh-oh, are you catching a cold? Time for some good old chicken soup. Millions of parents and grandparents the world over swear by the magical powers of chicken broth. But for some people, it's much more than just hot soup — it's a miracle cure for the common cold. This golden broth has been a favorite cold remedy since the twelfth century, but can a simple hot liquid made from poultry really cure your cold?

YOU DECIDE

Although there's no scientific proof that eating chicken soup can cure the common cold, it does help sick people feel a little better. When you have a cold, mucus builds up and clogs your sinuses, which can make it difficult to breathe. Chicken soup has been found to contain a mucus-thinning amino acid known as cysteine. Some researchers believe that this amino acid in chicken soup speeds up the movement of mucus in your nose so that it runs out faster, taking the virus with it. By the way, break it gently to Grandma when you tell her that researchers at the University of Nebraska found that store-bought canned chicken soup works just as well as the homemade stuff.

A chicken can live without its head.

What kind of a birdbrain would believe this one?
How can a living creature survive
without its head?

TRUE

Hard to believe, but it's true! "Mike the Headless Chicken" was a rooster that belonged to a farmer by the name of Olsen in Fruita, Colorado. On September 10, 1945, Mr. Olsen went out to the barn, chose a chicken for a family dinner that evening and chopped off its head, but left most of the brain stem attached. Well, it seems Mike wasn't interested in being served up for dinner that night, because even without his head attached to his body, the fearless chicken survived. After realizing what he had done, Mr. Olsen felt sorry for the headless rooster and fed him using an eyedropper. Mike went on to live an incredible 18 months after his beheading and even made it into the Guinness World Records in 2002 as the longest surviving headless chicken. Although not all chickens are super-chickens like Mike, a chicken will often stagger around without its noggin for a short while because the brain stem, which is often left partially attached, still controls the chicken's reflexes.

Bright sunlight can make you sneeze.

The sun provides us with warmth, energy and light, and makes our food crops grow. But how the heck can we be expected to believe that something so big and magnificent, something that is 150 million kilometers (93 million miles) away — or 149 597 870 kilometers (92 955 807 miles) to be exact — can cause us to sneeze? I mean, come on, doesn't the sun deserve more respect than being just another reason for saying "Pass the tissue, please"?

TRUE

Yep, the all-powerful ruler of the skies can make you sneeze. In fact, it's not just the sun that's to blame for these sneeze attacks; any bright light can set off your honker. This sneezing condition can be called everything from sun-sneezing to photic sneeze reflex (PSR) to ACHOO syndrome (Autosomal Dominant Compelling Helio-ophthalmic Outburst). It seems to affect 25 percent of the population, and no one really knows why it happens. Specialists at Stanford University School of Medicine in the United States think that it's kind of like a bad connection in the brain. A nerve called the trigeminal nerve causes us to sneeze. When people with ACHOO syndrome look at a bright light or the sun, the optic nerve in their eyes triggers the trigeminal nerve, causing them to sneeze. Strange, eh? The light bugs your eyes and that bugs your nose and that makes you sneeze. The ACHOO syndrome does run in families. So if Grandma or Grandpa start sneezing during your walk on a sunny afternoon in the park, you'd better have enough tissue on hand for the whole family!

Food Fallacies

Recipes for disaster?
Either it's good for you, it could kill you
or it might just give you gas. No matter
what you put in your mouth, adults will
have something to say about it.
Whether you believe what they claim
or not, this chapter will leave
you with a lot of food for thought.

You can still eat it as long as it's been on the floor for only five seconds.

So you're chowing down on a mouthwatering plate of french fries when you accidentally drop your last delicious fry on the kitchen floor. Using your super-human powers, you scoop it up faster than you can say "Fry-man to the rescue." You blow off the cooties, and as you're about to plop the yummy snack into your mouth, your dog, Spike, waddles across the kitchen floor for what must be the twentieth time that day. Spike licks the ketchup off the floor and looks up at you lovingly as you swallow. Bon appétit! Yep, turns out you just ate a whole lot of yuk!

According to food scientists at Clemson University, you should forget about the five-second rule and pretend you never heard of the three-second rule; in fact, it's probably not even safe to follow a one-second rule. In a recent study, Clemson researchers purposely contaminated several surfaces with salmonella, a kind of germ that can invade our bodies and make us sick. These tiny one-celled creatures eat up nutrients and energy and spread toxins through our bodies. As part of the study, the scientists dropped pieces of bologna and bread onto the infested surfaces for five seconds or more. After just five seconds, both foods had already picked up as many as 1800 bacteria, and the food that was left for as long as 60 seconds had up to 10 times that amount. So Rule #1: Don't eat food off the floor because every second counts!

Eating fish makes you smarter.

There are many benefits to eating fish. Many of these creatures from the deep are rich in omega-3 fatty acids, which are important in helping prevent arthritis and heart disease. In addition, these fatty acids are also considered brain food, especially for growing young minds like yours. But can eating these cold-blooded, aquatic vertebrates really make you smarter?

Nutritionists have studied the benefits of a healthy diet that includes fish and have found promising but not conclusive results. Our brain cells and our bodies crave polyunsaturated fatty acids, the good kind of fat — omega-3 fatty acids, which our bodies cannot make naturally. So by feeding your brain more of the good fatty acids, you get better-working brain cells. The experts agree that the fats found in cold-water fish such as sardines, salmon, mackerel and fresh tuna are important for normal brain development. Their studies have found that cultures whose diets include fish have a lower risk of developing brain-related diseases. But it still can't be proven that eating fish makes you smarter. So I guess you'd better get studying for that math quiz, 'cause chomping down on that pack of fish sticks isn't going to help you pass, now is it?

If you swallow a watermelon seed, a watermelon will grow inside your stomach.

Watermelon is one of the best things about summertime. But there's one drawback to eating this hot-weather treat — those annoying little black seeds. They are impossible to avoid and even harder to get rid of as you try to swallow the juicy red melon. Maybe you're a tough kid and not afraid of a little seed or two going down the wrong way. But be honest. Later, when you are lying in bed and your stomach starts to ache, do you imagine the roots of the seeds starting to wrap around your guts?

FALSE

Eating a few watermelon seeds doesn't mean a watermelon can actually grow in your stomach. In reality, you've probably swallowed quite a few seeds in your lifetime. This fruit that's 92 percent water contains about half a cup of seeds, but even if you swallowed most of them, they wouldn't grow inside you. In some very rare cases, the seeds can get stuck in your appendix or damage your intestines, but they can't grow inside your stomach. Dr. Gordon Rogers, a horticultural expert, even tried to grow seeds on purpose in his lab by matching the same conditions of the human stomach and digestive system. But Rogers's green thumb failed, and no matter how hard he tried, the seeds wouldn't grow. Rogers concluded that the seeds need moisture, the right temperature and oxygen in order to grow, which means your tummy just won't do.

Eating carrots can improve your eyesight, especially your night vision.

Is it true that eating these orange spearlike veggies will give you super vision? If you had a time machine, you could travel to the past and ask the German soldiers who served during the Second World War. The British military fooled the Germans into believing that they fed their troops lots of carrots to improve their eyesight during night missions. The British were actually trying to hide their new invention called radar that helped them track enemy planes at night, but the German military leaders took the carrot bait and had their pilots eating as many carrots as they could dig up. So what do you think happened? Did the carrot-eating German soldiers see any better at night?

Scientists today would probably tell you that the British weren't that far off from the truth about what carrots can do for your eyesight. But before you order a truckload of carrots and upset bunnies everywhere, keep reading. Eating carrots won't improve your eyesight, but it can help maintain the sight you have. Carrots are rich in beta-carotene, a natural chemical found in orange fruits and vegetables that helps keep the clear cornea (the outer membrane of the eye) healthy. It just so happens that our bodies turn beta-carotene into vitamin A, a very important nutrient for maintaining good eyesight. Not getting enough vitamin A can cause night blindness, and an extreme lack of vitamin A can even cause complete

blindness. So, what if you hate carrots? Don't worry, you can still get the vitamin A you need from eating lots of green leafy vegetables and other orange-colored fruits and vegetables. But watch out! If you eat too many carrots, the beta-carotene can build up in your bloodstream, making your skin look orange.

Wait an hour after eating before you go swimming, or you'll get a cramp and drown.

Whether you're at the lake or in a pool, swimming is one of the greatest ways to spend a hot afternoon. The next best thing has got to be munching away on some delicious favorites such as hot dogs, burgers and chips. Once your tummy's full, it's back into the water for you. But then you hear your mom's voice begging you not to go swimming so soon after you've eaten or you'll drown. You step back from the water's edge, safe once again from the jaws of death. But is she right?

Don't let Mom scare you out of the water — you're a born fish or maybe even a future Olympic gold medalist! Okay, that might be stretching it a bit, but it seems that stretching things is probably how this white lie got started in the first place. What's true is that during the digestive process, a lot of blood travels to the stomach to help digest the food you've just eaten, which causes it to temporarily flow away from the muscles. The reduced oxygen levels can cause muscle cramps in your arms or legs, which can make it difficult to swim. But no case of drowning has been blamed on a full stomach. Even the American Red Cross, the organization that has taught millions of people how to swim, doesn't warn against swimming after eating. So if you decide to pig out just before you take a dip, you might want to wait a bit so that you don't feel uncomfortable, but there's no scientific proof that says you need to wait an hour or you'll drown.

Eating Pop Rocks candy and drinking a soda pop at the same time will make your stomach explode!

What an explosive idea, a candy and soda pop combination that won't only rot your teeth — it will blow your guts out! When this popular candy first hit the market, rumors spread that eating Pop Rocks while drinking a soda pop had killed a boy in the United States. No way, you say? Well then how come the company who originally made the candy stopped selling it for almost 10 years?

FALSE

Relax, candy addicts. It won't hurt you to combine these two mouthwatering treats. In fact, the candy was so popular, even with all the false rumors being spread around, that in 1985 Kraft Foods bought the secret recipe from General Foods. It knew the candies weren't dangerous and that kids everywhere loved to eat the exploding sensations, so Kraft decided to change the name from Pop Rocks to Action Candy just because the original name had made the candy difficult to sell. Today, Pop Rocks are back on candy store shelves where they belong, and they've even gone back to their original name. But in 2006, the legend of the "exploding kid" was reborn. This time, the deadly combination was said to be soda pop and Mentos, the chewy mints, and rumor had it that a kid from Brazil had died eating the two together. Turns out this story was just somebody's wild imagination, too.

Beans, beans, the magical fruit, the more you eat, the more you toot. The more you toot, the better you feel, so eat your beans at every meal!

To start with, why would anyone tell kids that beans are a fruit? Everyone knows that beans are in fact a vegetable — right? And why would parents have their kid sing a song about tooting? If you've ever sat next to a real wicked tooter, or been trapped underneath the covers in a deadly gas explosion by someone you thought was your friend, then you know there's nothing about a real stinker that could make you feel better. So why would grown adults choose to pass along this silly rhyme about beans and farting?

TRUE

Actually, this funny little rhyme about the benefit of letting off a little steam is true on both accounts. Not only are beans a fruit, but they also really do make you fart, and farting really does make you feel better. Beans make us fart because they contain sugars that our bodies have a hard time digesting. When these sugars meet up with the bacteria in our intestines, our system goes crazy, resulting in an intestinal explosion — P.U. The release of this built-up gas, or farting, is good for you because these digestive gases have to escape, and what better exit route than your butt!

If you want curly hair, eat your bread crusts.

This saying may have originated three hundred years ago, in Europe. Back then, people who had curly hair were seen as being more successful than those with straight hair. Somehow, a rumor got started that eating bread crusts made your hair curly, so everyone who wanted to look successful devoured every bit of bread they could get their hands on. But did it really work back then? And could it work for you today? Or did the rich of yesteryear just have so much time on their hands that they sat around counting their gold coins and curling their own hair, tricking the less fortunate straight-haired for generations to come?

FALSE

This sounds like a hair-raising idea, but it's just not true. Generations of parents most likely passed on this white lie to get their kids to finish their sandwiches. So go ahead and remove those pesky brown edges that just seem to get in the way when you're trying to bite into your sandwich. But keep this in mind: Although crusts won't make your hair curly or make you any more successful, they do have other health benefits. Turns out the brown of the crust, the hard, crunchy part, may contain more antioxidants, a substance that helps prevent cancer, than the softer part of the bread. So you can cut off the crusts if you want, but feed them to someone you care about.

Eating fried foods can cause acne.

This one is no laughing matter if you've ever had to deal with acne. Whether you call them pimples, zits or spots, having these pesky little sores popping up all over your face can be a real bummer. So where do these little blobs of misery come from? Could they really be caused by all the yummy things kids love to eat, such as chips, onion rings and french fries? Please say it isn't so.

Numerous scientific studies have all come to the same conclusion — acne is not caused by eating fried foods. Pimples appear on your skin when a pore (that's a tiny hole in the skin) becomes blocked. Each pore contains a tiny hair and oil glands at the base. The cells that line the pores are discarded quickly during puberty. For some people, the cells and the oil stick together and form a sebum, which plugs the pore and causes your skin to break out. Acne may also be hereditary, which means it may have been passed along to you from either your mom or your dad's side of the family. Combine your family history with puberty and you've got a face full of nasty visitors. But just because what you eat doesn't cause acne doesn't mean you have an excuse to turn into a junk food junkie. Eating a variety of nutritious foods is still the best way to keep your body, and skin, healthy and strong.

Animal Tales

More fun than a barrel of monkeys?
Whether they're potential germ spreaders,
wart-causing amphibians, or giant baby-
carrying birds, the world of animals
breeds some odd adult beliefs.
Be forewarned, some of these
sayings will drive you batty!

Don't touch that toad, or you'll get warts!

The fact that these bumpy-looking amphibians appear to be covered in warts has caused them much ridicule among their pond peers. But before you judge these swamp-dwellers for their unsightly bumps, keep in mind that their wart-covered bodies are actually Mother Nature's clever design to help keep them camouflaged in their natural habitat. But can their warty disguise be passed on to humans?

FALSE

Okay, so maybe toads aren't the prettiest creatures on Earth, unless of course you're another toad. But if you have to kiss a frog to find a real prince, then what's so bad about touching a toad? Nothing, really. The idea that toads cause warts may be a simple case of mistaken identity. Warts on people aren't actually caused by getting up close and personal with their favorite toad, they're caused by human viruses of the human papillomavirus (HPV) family. The virus responsible for causing warts can enter the skin through a recent cut or scratch and cause a rapid growth of cells on the outer layer of the skin. You can pick up HPV from touching anything someone with a wart has touched, such as a towel, or a surface, such as a sink or a shower floor. But some people do have an allergy to the oily substance most toads secrete from their skin, produced by poison glands located on their backs. It can cause them to break out in bumps that look like warts, but it's just another case of mistaken identity.

An elephant never forgets.

The first question you have to ask yourself is this: Forgets what? What's so important that an elephant would never forget? Always look both ways before crossing the street? No. Don't count your chickens before they hatch? Nah. Always remember to wash behind your ears? Maybe. Seems the origin of this phrase comes from observations made over the years by scientists and animal trainers alike, but is there any truth to it?

TRUE The largest land animal in the world really does have a great memory to match its size. Elephants have very large brains, which allow them lots of room for memory storage. In addition, elephants live a long time, some 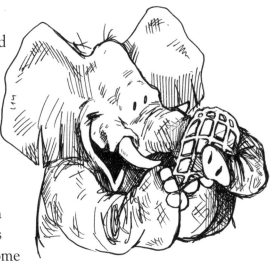 well into their seventies, so their learning is acquired over years. Researchers have found that elephants remember not only other elephants they've met, but also human beings they've had relationships with. Even more incredible is the fact that many years may pass, decades even, and the elephants still remember familiar members of their species and people they once knew. So the next time you can't remember your science teacher's name, ask the elephant sitting next to you — he'll remember.

A dog's mouth is cleaner than a human's.

If you love your dog, which I'm sure you do, then you're very familiar with the odor that comes from your bowwow's mouth. Rover not only eats with his mouth, as we all do, he also raids garbage cans, chews on dead squirrels and uses his tongue as toilet paper. There has to be over a billion germs swimming around in his saliva, just waiting to land on you the next time he slobbers. So with all the disgusting uses a dog has for its tongue, how could it be cleaner than yours?

FALSE

The answer is no, sort of. See, you can't really compare a dog's mouth to a human's. "It's like comparing apples and oranges," says Professor Colin Harvey from the University of Pennsylvania's School of Veterinary Medicine. Both mouths, human and canine, are full of germs, but the germs are quite different from one another. Many of the bacteria found in a dog's mouth are species specific, meaning they can't harm humans — unless the dog has rabies, and you won't want to smooch a dog that has rabies. But, generally humans are immune to most dog germs. On the other hand, human germs can harm humans. So a bite from your little sister could be more dangerous than a bite from a dog's mouth full of dog germs. So go ahead and give your pooch a smooch, just try to keep your germs to yourself!

Animals can predict natural disasters.

Have you ever noticed that just before it rains, your dog wants to come inside, or that birds seem to disappear before a storm? Many people, some scientists included, believe that animals have a "sixth sense" or a natural ability to predict bad weather. But can a dog or a flock of birds really predict a natural disaster? If this is true, maybe it's time we stopped watching the weather channel and started getting our weather reports from local zoos or from the animals in our own backyards.

YOU DECIDE

It seems that no one really has a clear answer when it comes to animals predicting the weather. During the horrible tsunami that struck Southeast Asia on December 26, 2004, more than two hundred thousand people died, but many animals survived. Although it's not scientifically proven, many people believe that the animals had some sort of early warning that the storm was coming. Researchers who study animal behavior believe that animals can pick up early infrasonic, or lower frequency, sounds (such as the pulses in the earth created by earthquakes and storms) better than humans can, and head for safety early. But the United States Geological Survey, a federal source for science about Earth, its resources, natural hazards and environment, says that even though there have been cases of unusual animal behavior before an earthquake, no scientific connection has been made. I don't know about you, but if I see animals behaving strangely, I'm heading for cover!

A falling cat will always land on its feet.

Here, kitty, kitty, kitty. Have you ever tried to rescue a cat stuck in a tree? Chances are it will scurry farther away each time you try to grab it. And it's no wonder cats don't think they need to be rescued. These furry, four-legged felines are said to have nine lives. But are these purring fur balls really that well coordinated that they're guaranteed to always land on their feet when they fall?

YOU DECIDE

While it's not true that cats always land on their feet, especially if they fall more than a few stories, it is true that they can recover from lower falls. If these wiry animals fall a short distance, one or two floors off a building, they can almost always right themselves and land on their feet. The exceptional construction of a cat's skeleton is what makes this possible. Cats don't have collarbones, and their backbones allow them more movement than most other animals. These small changes in their skeletal frame allow free movement of their front legs so they can easily bend and rotate their bodies — especially in midair! This quick movement allows a cat to turn itself right-side up when it is falling and land on its paws — Meow! Now that's impressive, pussycat. But don't let these feline acrobats fool you. Cats can be seriously injured and even fatally wounded from a fall of two or more floors.

Groundhogs can predict the coming of spring.

You've obviously heard of Groundhog Day, when if a groundhog sees its shadow, we are doomed to six more weeks of winter. But did you know that this tradition actually began in Germany, with badgers instead of groundhogs? When German settlers arrived in America in the 1700s, many of them brought their badger-watching tradition with them. Since they couldn't find badgers, they began to use groundhogs as their spring detectors, instead. This method of predicting spring soon caught on among other farmers, and one groundhog became so famous that he was named Punxsutawney Phil, after the town he lived in. Canada has its own famous king of spring, Wiarton Willie, also named after his hometown in Ontario. All this tradition and fame sounds great, but do these underground dwellers really know their stuff?

FALSE

I know. It's hard to believe that groundhogs (a.k.a. woodchucks, land beavers, whistlepigs) can't really tell it's spring, especially with all the fame they've received over the years. But the facts speak for themselves. It turns out that over the 120 years that Punxsutawney Phil has been in the prediction business, he's been right only 39 percent of the time. Hey, Phil, time to look for another day job, maybe as a hole-digging rodent? In fact, groundhogs spend a lot of their time digging very impressive tunnels underground. It's estimated that an average groundhog can dig up to 320 kilograms (700 pounds) of earth while preparing its burrow. These fabulous diggers, with short powerful limbs and thick curved claws, are dirt removal specialists.

The stork brings babies.

Have you ever sat outside on a clear, warm summer night and stared up at the beautiful sky? Sure you have. And as you tried to count stars or spot a shooting star, you've probably seen a few storks fly by with babies swinging from cloth cradles in their beaks. Sure you have. What? Wait a sec! Do you really expect anyone to believe that you've actually seen these large white birds gliding through the sky carrying babies? It's not possible, is it? Could these swamp- and pond-dwelling birds really be Mother Nature's baby mail service?

Of course storks don't bring babies — but you already knew that, right? It seems that this tale of giant white birds dropping newborn babies off to their parents was made up to save adults from the embarrassing sex talk. This idea of the stork bringing babies first originated in Scandinavia and was used in many fairy tales by the famous writer Hans Christian Andersen. He wrote two stories that featured the stork, "The Storks" published in 1838 and "What the Moon Saw" in 1840. And the stork's habit of nesting on warm chimneys and stealing clothes off clotheslines to stuff into their nests had people thinking they were stuffing babies down the chimney. Move over, Santa, one bouncing baby boy coming down! So now you know the truth. You were found in a cabbage patch. Now go and ask your parents to explain it.

Bats fly blind.

Does the thought of a bat flying at you drive you batty? If so, you're not alone. Bats are probably one of the most misunderstood animals in the world. Turns out they are actually very helpful to humankind. These creatures of the night swoop through the air with one thing on their minds, and no, it's not to suck your blood — it's food. One bat alone can eat anywhere from six hundred to a thousand mosquitoes and other pesky insects in just one hour! But are these small bug-eating machines really flying blind?

FALSE

Now you've got one less thing to be freaked out about when it comes to bats. According to "Bat Man" Paul Faure, a neuroethologist (someone who studies how animals' brains affect their behavior), bats are not blind. In fact, they have good eyesight, very good hearing and an excellent sense of smell. Many experts believe that the idea that bats are blind may have come from two misconceptions about the creatures. First, they rely more on their incredible sonar than their eyes to navigate through dark areas and to avoid obstacles. They navigate at night by making high-pitched noises that humans can't hear. When the sounds bounce back off of objects, such as trees or houses, bats are able to form a picture in their brains of what is around them and what they need to avoid. And second, if you watch them fly through the air, swooping and diving aimlessly for bugs, they appear to be flying blind. But have no fear, these mammals that come in more than a thousand species know exactly where they're headed — to lunch!

Ostriches bury their heads in the sand when they're scared.

Why not just stick your head in the ground and hope that whatever is scaring you goes away? Well, if you're the largest species of bird on the planet, hiding just your head not only seems a little odd, but it would also look pretty silly. Before you write off the ostrich as a dodo bird, however, keep in mind its incredible history. Ostriches have been here since dinosaurs roamed Earth. Paleontologists, scientists who study dinosaur remains, believe that the ostrich could be related to T. Rex! So maybe this simple trick of hiding your head in the sand works. After all, they've managed to outlast most of their enemies.

These giant birds are no dummies. Their first instinct when frightened is the same as yours and mine — they run! And these large, flightless birds can reach speeds of up to 74 kilometers per hour (46 miles per hour), allowing them to outrun most of their predators. But when outrunning their enemies isn't an option, these clever birds simply hit the dirt! That's right — they flop to the ground and remain as still as possible, with their heads and necks flat out in front of them. Because their head feathers are tan colored, they match the ground and from far away it looks like their heads have disappeared into the sand. Ostrich experts believe that's how the myth that these birds bury their heads in the sand when they're scared got started. When actually it's just an illusion or a trick of the eye.

Lemmings will follow each other right off a cliff.

These reddish-brown little creatures that are more guinea pig than mouse seem to have figured out how to survive life in the harsh North. They survive the winters by burrowing in underground snow tunnels that they dig out themselves. But every three to five years, the lemming population explodes up to five hundred times its number! Then, mysteriously, the lemming population crashes to near extinction. So where are all the lemmings going?

FALSE

For years, people thought that lemmings jump off cliffs as a way of controlling their population. This idea was reinforced by a Walt Disney documentary movie called *White Wilderness*, part of the studio's True Life Adventure series, made in 1958. It showed the little brown fur balls scurrying in huge packs toward a rocky cliff, plunging to their deaths in the waters below. But it was all fake, says Charles Krebs, an ecologist who has been studying the lemming population since he was a kid. Seems these crafty moviemakers took a large group of lemmings from their Arctic home to Alberta, Canada, and chased them off a cliff as they filmed. So for years, people believed that these rodents were just a depressed version of Mickey Mouse. Not so, say researchers. The lemming population explodes every four years in Scandinavia. When the tundra gets too crowded, some lemmings leave home. Being a little dumb, they sometimes fall off cliffs as they search for new homes — but never on purpose!

A mother bird will reject her babies if they have been touched by humans.

You're walking along the street on a beautiful summer afternoon when you spot a tiny, feathered creature abandoned on the sidewalk. You look around for help, but no one's there. Looking up, you spot the little fellow's nest and realize that somehow junior has left the flock too soon. Now what do you do? Should you scoop up baby bird and place him safely back where he came from? Or does that nagging voice in your head tell you that you could be doing him more harm than good? You know the voice. You can hear your dad warning you, loud and clear, "Don't touch that baby bird or its mother will reject it!" But is he right?

FALSE

Quit your worrying. The little chipper's mother is probably watching you and her wee babe, and she isn't going to let him starve to death, or peck your eyes out. She most likely pushed him out of the nest because she's teaching him how to fly. So it's probably best to leave the feathered flyer in the very capable hands of his mother. The idea that female birds reject their young once they've been touched by humans probably came about because adults realized that handling birds wasn't such a good thing. The thought that a mother bird can smell a human on her young is just not true. "Most birds have a poorly developed sense of smell," says Michael Mace, bird curator at San Diego Zoo's Wild Animal Park. "They won't notice a human scent." But Mace warns there is one exception: the vulture, who can sniff quite well. But you probably wouldn't want to pick up a vulture's baby anyway!

Parentisms: An Overview

Throughout this book, we've tried to explain why adults say the things they do. But even after all our research, in the end there are just some things that can't be explained. This section of the book is about the truly unexplainable things adults say to kids, which we like to refer to as "parentisms." How many of these wacky sayings have you heard your parents use?

- A little "birdy" told me!

- Talking to you is like talking to a brick wall.

- Because I said so, that's why.

- I can see everything you do. I've got eyes in the back of my head.

- This room looks like a tornado went through it!

- Do as I say, not as I do.

- Do you think I'm made of money?

- Do you think your socks are going to pick up themselves?

- How do you know you don't like it if you haven't tried it?

- Over my dead body!

- Put that down! You don't know where it's been!

- Always wear clean underwear in case you get in an accident.

- So it's raining? You're not sugar — you won't melt.

- I wasn't born yesterday, you know.

- There's enough dirt in those ears to grow potatoes!

- You must think rules were made to be broken.

- I'll treat you like an adult when you start acting like one.

- I'm going to give you until the count of three ...

- If I ever hear you say that again, I'll wash your mouth out with soap.

- What do you think this is, a hotel?

- If you can't say something nice, don't say anything at all.

- If you don't clean your plate, you won't get any dessert.

- If you're too full to finish your dinner, you're too full for dessert.

- The apple doesn't fall far from the tree.

- I'm not running a taxi service.

- No, I don't know where your socks are, it's not my day to watch them!

- You will eat it, and you will like it!

- Turn off that light. Do you think we own the electric company?

- Were you born in a barn? Close the door — and don't slam it!

- Who said life was going to be easy?

- It's no use crying over spilt milk.

- You can't judge a book by its cover.

- You made your bed, now lie in it.

- You should have that phone surgically implanted in your ear.

- You'd forget your head if it wasn't attached to your shoulders!

- When I was your age, I had to walk 10 miles through the snow to get to school.